ANTIETAM

THE SOLDIERS' BATTLEFIELD

A Self-Guided Mini-Tour

by
John Michael Priest

WHITE MANE PUBLISHING COMPANY, INC.

This White Mane Publishing Company, Inc. publication
was printed by
Beidel Printing House, Inc.
63 West Burd Street
Shippensburg, PA 17257 USA

The acid-free paper used in this book meets the guidelines for permanence and durability of the Committee on Production Guidelines for Book Longevity of the Council on Library Resources.

For a complete list of available publications
please write
White Mane Publishing Company, Inc.
P.O. Box 152
Shippensburg, PA 17257 USA

Library of Congress Cataloging-in-Publication Data

Priest, John Michael, 1949-
    Antietam : the soldiers' battlefield : a self-guided mini-tour /
by John Michael Priest.
       p.   cm.
    ISBN 0-942597-67-2 : $6.95
    1. Antietam National Battlefield (Md.)--Guidebooks.   2. Antietam,
Battle of, Md., 1862.   I. Title.
E474.65.P92   1994
973.7'336--dc20   94-10648
                                                  CIP

PRINTED IN THE UNITED STATES OF AMERICA

INTRODUCTION:

Antietam National Battlefield remains one of the easiest of the National Battlefield Parks to visit, either by foot or by car. This book may be used independently or in conjunction with the battlefield audio cassette tour and/or the park's self guided auto tour. The cassette tapes provide both the strategic perspectives and the grand tactical aspects of the fighting. The excerpts in this booklet are from *Antietam: The Soldiers' Battle* and are included so the visitor can gain a more personal understanding of the fighting from the perspectives of the actual participants.

CAUTIONARY NOTES:

When touring the battlefield in the spring and summer you will probably be attacked by gnats. They can be quite irksome. The area also abounds in ticks. While they are more than likely to be a nuisance to the hiker they can be picked up in any of the wooded or grassy areas of the park. Ground hog (woodchuck) holes can be found almost anywhere upon the field. Thus, visitors should watch where they step. Wasps tend to nest in the ends of the iron rail hand rails down by Burnside Bridge which is why one's hands should not be placed on the ends of the rails without checking them first. Antietam is a rural battlefield. There are snakes upon the field; for example, black snakes have been seen down at Burnside Bridge. There are also copperheads in the area. Follow the park guidelines and stay upon the marked trails and paths. In compliance with park policy do not climb on monuments or the cannon barrels and wheels.

Most of the places in the park along the tour route are accessible to physically challenged individuals. The hardest place to reach is tour Stop Nine — Burnside Bridge.

THE BOOKLET FORMAT:

Each tour stop number in this booklet is numbered to coincide with the identical stop on the battlefield's self conducted tour. Maps taken from *Antietam: The Soldiers' Battle* are on even numbered pages and correspond to specific stops on the audio-cassette tour. Excerpts from *Antietam: The Soldiers' Battle*, describing incidents which occurred at or near those locations, are on odd numbered pages. Note: All maps are oriented so that the direction "South" is at the bottom of the map parallel with the map caption. The scales on the maps are in 100-yard increments.

STOP ONE — Part One

   With your back to the Dunker Church door, face the Hagerstown Pike and scan the ridge across from you. To your left is the Maryland Monument. To your immediate front is the monument to Hector Tyndale's Ohio brigade. On the ridge behind it is the eagle topped New York Monument. Farther to the right is the flag draped 20th New York Monument. Coming back toward Tyndale's monument is the four gun battery to represent Colonel Stephen D. Lee's artillery position. The excerpt and the accompanying map portray the action between dawn and 6:20 A.M.

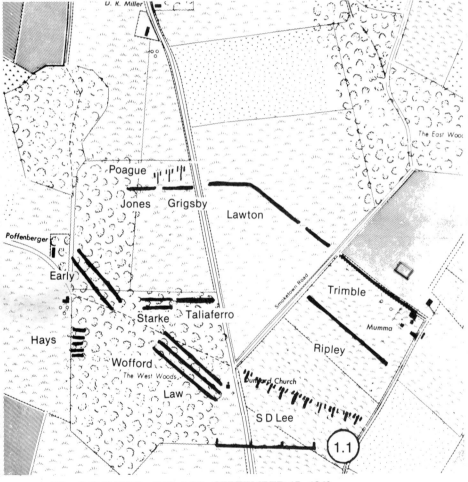

(Map 1.1) DAWN - 6:20 A.M., SEPTEMBER 17, 1862
The Confederate troop disposition on the northern end of the field before the first Federal infantry assault.

Captain Parker's gunners, near the Dunker Church, were too enveloped in the smoke of their own pieces and of the incoming rounds to notice whether or not Jordan's section, which had unlimbered north of the Smoketown Road, had fallen silent. His body shot through with adrenalin, Captain Parker darted his horse from one end of the battery to the other. All the while, he exhorted his men to respond to the Yankee fire with all the energy they could muster. During the excitement, the captain singled out Corporal James Darden, with whom he shared a political and spiritual affinity and whom he considered to be the coolest man in his battery. While running from gun to gun, Parker screamed at the corporal, "If I am killed, tell my wife I was never happier in my life." In the ecstacy of the moment, the normally reserved, close mouthed officer revealed a darker side of his personality — his blood lust.

William Parker's battery was getting plenty of Yankee attention. It seemed as if every field piece of the entire Army of the Potomac had trained upon his people. The enemy had gotten range with the first round they fired from one of the big guns across the Antietam. The knoll became an inferno. The sky burst and thundered with successive concussions. It rolled and hissed with shell fragments. His boys started to drop with disconcerting regularity, their pitiful cries piercing the sulfuric cloud which shrouded their position. Stray rounds were also taking men out.

Fifteen year old Davey Brown fell with a ball through the leg. Corporal Newell was dead. Lieutenant Parkinson was down with a shattered knee. Captain Parker dismounted and hurriedly operated on his prize officer in an effort to save his life. He wanted him back to his guns. Bill Cook got leg shot — a minor wound. John Turnbridge caught one through the hand. Horses pitched and screamed, frantic from the smell of blood.

STOP ONE — *Part Two*

Face north and walk down to Confederate Avenue. To your left (west) on the top of the hill you will see the statue of a Federal color bearer. Ascend the hill to the front of the statue and face left again (south). The Hagerstown Pike will now be on your left as well as the Dunker Church. The following reading describes the action around the Dunker Church from 9:00 A.M. to 9:30 A.M., immediately before the collapse of the Federal position in the West Woods.

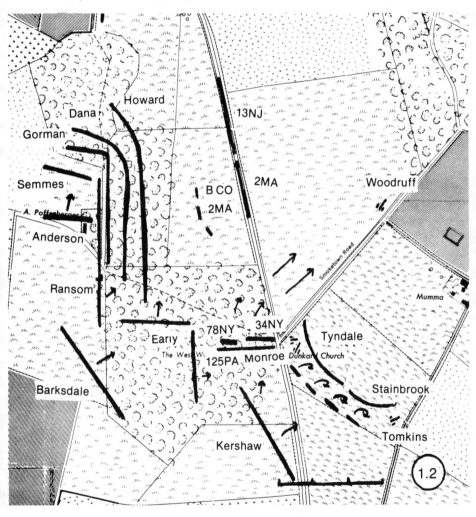

(Map 1.2) 9:00 A.M. - 9:30 A.M., SEPTEMBER 17, 1862
The collapse of the Dunker Church and the envelopment of Sedgwick's flank.

Meanwhile, the 125th Pennsylvania, a part of the 78th New York, and the 34th New York had taken about all of the beating they could handle. "Uncle John" Sedgwick rode away from his division to check on the situation at the Dunker Church, which he found untenable. He ordered Colonel James A. Suiter to pull the 34th New York out of the action, then he galloped away to turn Howard's left flank to face south. He triggered a holocaust.

The 34th New York and the 78th New York stampeded northeast, leaving the 125th Pennsylvania on its own to face the four Confederate brigades in its sector. Kershaw's and Early's Brigades pressed the line from the front and the right.

Captain Ulysses L. Huyette (B Co.) stormed into the 125th Pennsylvania. The Rebs were closing in on the Dunker Church. He could not hold them back. Colonel Higgins frantically looked about him. Seeing no Federal supports anywhere, he ordered the regiment to retreat. The men, at first, refused to comply. He sent Adjutant Johnston toward the right of the line with the order to pull out, but a bullet killed him before he could execute the command. Suddenly, the Rebel Yell echoed along the regiment's front. Colonel Higgins responded with an oath, but to no avail.

The Rebs were so close that they shouted at the Pennsylvanians to surrender. They ran, instead. The right of the line peeled back then disintegrated, dragging the left of the regiment with it, as the men, individually and in groups scattered toward the East Woods. Private Fred Gerhard (D Co.) did not get the word. He stayed in the woods long enough to shoot his last round before he trotted down the Smoketown Road. Miles Huyette (B Co.) received the shock of his life when he discovered himself standing alone near the Dunker Church with the Confederates less than fifty yards away. He made tracks toward Mumma's. Privates J. George Lincoln and C. James McDivett (both C Co.) dragged Michael Brenneman (C Co.) out of the fray at great risk to their own lives. The Confederates swarmed through the woods, shooting madly as they went. Federal soldiers scattered like quail. Having no time for the wounded, they left many of

9

them behind. Two rounds simultaneously cut down the Simpson brothers (H Co.). Randolph dropped with a bullet in the breast. The color sergeant, George, caught one in the temple. The colors went down repeatedly with five other members of the color guard, one of whom received five wounds before he gave them up. Fifteen year old Eugene Boblits (H Co.) snatched up the flag and carried it a short distance when a bullet knocked him down. Sergeant Walter Greenland (C Co.) took the standard from Boblits and bore it toward Mumma's.

Notes & Queries

STOP TWO

Use the parking area on the left as your reference for the following excerpt. The Joseph Poffenberger farm is to your left front as you face north. The entire farm served as a field hospital throughout the battle and afterward. You are parked on the tour road which on the adjacent map runs from "Anderson to Magilton." You are parked in the area somewhere near "2 WI." The North Woods at the time of the battle would be behind you to the south. The incident on the next page occurred just after dawn in the low ground to your left front.

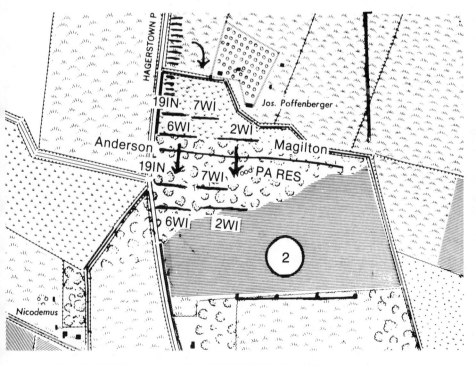

(Map 2) DAWN - 6:20 A.M., SEPTEMBER 17, 1862
The deployment of Gibbon's Brigade in the North Woods.

The Union soldiers littered their previous night's bivouacs with their playing cards which they quickly chucked to rid themselves of Satanic instruments. Major Rufus Dawes, second in command of the 6th Wisconsin (4/1/I), hurriedly organized his small regiment for the advance with the brigade. Small arms fire crackled to the south. In the distance, he heard the thunder of Parker's guns near the Dunker Church. His men got to their feet like the professionals they were supposed to be — including those who had gorged themselves on Samuel and Joseph Poffenberger's apples the evening before.

The brigade prepared to advance at the "common time" toward Meade's nervous Pennsylvania Reserves, who were posted in the North Woods, facing south. The Western regiments formed in columns of divisions (two companies on line). The 6th Wisconsin, with the 2nd Wisconsin to its immediate rear, placed its right flank against the post and rail fence on the eastern side of the Hagerstown Pike. The 7th Wisconsin, with the 19th Indiana to its rear, fell in behind the 2nd Wisconsin. Colonel Walter Phelps' small brigade (22nd, 24th, 30th, and 84th N.Y., and the 2nd U.S. Sharpshooters) then Marsena Patrick's New Yorkers finished out the column.

By the time they started to move out, Poague's Confederate battery rolled onto the hillcrest south of D. R. Miller's barn. At first, First Sergeant William H. Harris (B Co., 2nd WI) mistook it for one of their own batteries. The scream of incoming shells shattered that illusion. As the line stepped off, two exploded simultaneously in the thick fog above the center of the Iron Brigade. A third, probably a percussion shell, burst in the rear line of the 6th Wisconsin. Screams and moans rent the air as searing iron gouged a tremendous hole in the unsuspecting ranks. Captain David K. Noyes (A Co.) dropped with blood spurting from the stump where a foot had been. Their brigade commander, Brigadier General John Gibbon, anxiously watched the soldiers calmly drag the wounded away before going any farther. That single round struck down thirteen men. Lieutenant

Colonel Edward S. Bragg (6th WI) ordered his men to close ranks. As they advanced, parade like, toward the North Woods, the commands shifted into regimental fronts. The 2nd Wisconsin moved to the left of the 6th Wisconsin and the 7th Wisconsin filed left while the 19th Indiana moved into the open space next to the Hagerstown Pike. They left behind a number of dead, among them a terribly mangled soldier whose arms and legs were ripped from his body.

Notes & Queries

STOP THREE

The parking pull over is on your right as you turn onto Cornfield Avenue. During the time of the battle this area would have been in the East Woods (about one half of an inch to the left of the word "The" in "The East Woods"). The East Woods was open and clean, much like it is today. It did not impede troop movement or block visibility. Cornfield Avenue parallels the southern border of the Cornfield as it existed during the war.

The reading refers to some of the fighting which occurred to your left front as you face west along the tour road. The fighting continued across the horizon to your right front.

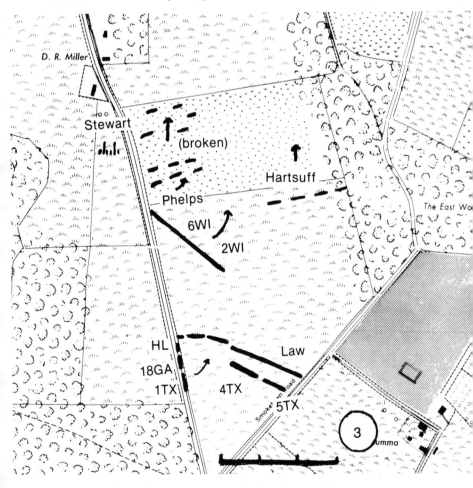

(Map 3) 6:25 A.M. - 7:00 A.M., SEPTEMBER 17, 1862
Hood's division thwarts the Federal charge from the Cornfield.

On the Federal right, near the Hagerstown Pike, the situation disintegrated from possible victory to a staggering rout. About half way through the clover field, the line abruptly halted. The Yankees' weapons were too fouled to use. Men had to pound the ramrods home to seat their shots.

A long, unbroken line of Confederates swarmed out from around the Dunker Church. They fired by files as they approached the trapped New Yorkers and Westerners on the western flank. Men fell like grass beneath a scythe.

A panicked soldier shrieked, "Now save who can."

Rifles clattered to the ground as shoulder straps and enlisted men alike raced back to Miller's corn. Private Silas Howard (E Co., 2nd US SS) who had been shot several times, including once through the chest, defiantly jerked the firing block from his Sharps rifle and hurled it as far as he could. Since he expected to die, he was not about to give the Rebs a serviceable weapon. Major Rufus Dawes (6th WI) felt a sharp sting on the back of his calf, but kept on running.

Hood's rugged Division (Law's and Wofford's Brigades), screaming like mad men, bolted into the high ground above S. D. Lee's Battalion and pressed for the Cornfield, while most of Starke's and Taliaferro's badly mauled units retreated to the West Woods. The soul chilling Rebel yell echoed across the smoke covered field as Hood's wild men charged across the bloodied ground between the Cornfield and the Smoketown Road. Law's men (the 2nd and 11th MS, and the 6th NC) moved toward the Federals in a northeasterly line, while his last regiment, the 4th Alabama, moved by the right flank down the Smoketown Road toward the East Woods.

The Texas Brigade (the 18th GA, Hampton's Legion, and the 1st, 4th, and 5th TX) came up, close upon its heels. About halfway through the field, Law halted his people to meet Hartsuff's volleys. The 4th and 5th Texas regiments, which were right behind the 11th Mississippi, nearly collided with its rear rank.

17

Lieutenant Colonel B. F. Carter (4th TX) immediately ordered his men prone and cautioned them not to fire until they could definitely identify the troops to their front as friend or foe. Lieutenant W. H. Sellers, Hood's aide, simultaneously made the 5th Texas lie down. The 18th Georgia, with Hampton's Legion and the 1st Texas raced across the Hagerstown Pike into the clover field. The Georgians triggered a rolling fusillade from their hips into the remnants of the 6th and 2nd Wisconsin, which had halted to deliver one more volley before disappearing into the Cornfield. The diminutive Hampton's Legion (seventy-seven effectives), as it brought up the left of the line to the eastern side of the Hagerstown Pike, ran directly into Lieutenant James Stewart's case rounds.

Notes & Queries

STOP FOUR — Part One

The parking area is on the right. When you pull into this stop you will be facing north. The reading describes the fighting from 7:00 to 7:20 A.M. between the Texas Brigade and the 1st Corps counterattack against the Cornfield. The action occurred along the northern and the western boundaries of the Cornfield, to your front and left respectively.

(Map 4.1) 7:00 A.M. - 7:20 A.M., SEPTEMBER 17, 1862
The decimation of the Texas Brigade in the Cornfield.

Lieutenant Colonel P. A. Work (1st TX) found himself in a very bad fix. Almost half of his regiment was scattered through the corn. Rifle fire was coming in from the front and both flanks. In the confusion, he sent his adjutant, Sergeant W. Shropshire (D Co.) to find General Hood and get permission to retire. A volley from the unbroken 9th, 11th, and 12th Pennsylvania Reserves countermanded that decision. The 1st Texas began to inch its way south toward the swale east of the Dunker Church. As the regiment's fourth color bearer, Jimmy Malone (K Co.) stepped to the rear a burst of musketry killed him. The colonel saw six men dash after the colors. He saw the flag raised momentarily only to disappear in the corn and the smoke as the regiment kept moving rearward.

Of the two hundred twenty-six men the Colonel led into the Cornfield, only forty came away unhurt. Many of the wounded fell into Federal hands. Lieutenant Tom Sanford (M Co.) was among them, downed with a bullet in the thigh from which he bled to death.

The four Perry boys in E Company did not get away either. Early O. Perry died in the corn and his brother H. Eugene dropped with a wound. Clinton Perry, who was not related to either of the other two, perished, while his brother, S. F. "Bose" Perry was shot but not killed. Captain F. S. Bass (E Co.) sacrificed eighteen of his twenty-one men in the Cornfield.

Not one of the six men who chased after the colors returned. The 1st Texas, in every sense of the phrase, was "used up."

To the left rear of the 1st Texas, Private Elliott Welch (Hampton's Legion) regained consciousness. His head felt strange. He slowly realized that his right eye would not open, that his right ear was filled with blood and that he was lying in a pool of his own blood. His rifle was to one side of him and his cap to the other.

He numbly examined the kepi, heedless of the bullets which whistled around him. The shell fragment had ripped the lining apart inside, but had left the outside material in one piece. He later scrawled home, "It is really a mercy I was not torn to pieces."

Alone in his pain, he dazedly staggered rearward.

When Lieutenant Colonel Gary (H. L.) observed the 7th Wisconsin, the 19th Indiana, the 21st New York, and the 35th New York making a bee line for his position, he realized that his twenty-two men could not defend the Pike. They skedaddled.

Lieutenant Colonel S. Z. Ruff (18th GA) and his few men noticed the four Yankee regiments pressing toward his left flank also. He quit the field with his seventy-five remaining soldiers by running the gauntlet of fire along the Hagerstown Pike toward the West Woods.

Lieutenant Colonel Carter (4th TX) had posted his outfit in the Pike along the inside sections of the fence which bordered the road. His men had taken severe fire for what seemed like hours but actually had been only minutes. The air was filled with lead.

His wounded crawled in among the boulders which flanked the road on both sides, trying to protect themselves from more harm. The colonel could hear them crying as they were repeatedly struck by ricocheting bullets.

Notes & Queries

STOP FOUR — Part Two

Face north across the rail fence to your front. You will see the D. R. Miller farm house to your left on your side of the Hagerstown Pike. A long, low ridge extends from the ground behind the house to your right and the East Woods. That is the position held by the 3rd Wisconsin and the 27th Indiana. The reading on the next page describes the final minutes of action in the Cornfield.

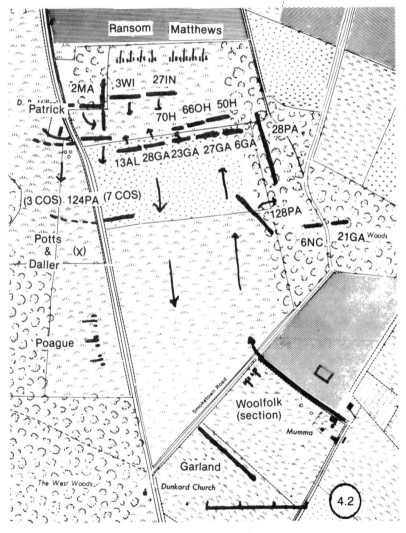

(Map 4.2) 8:00 A.M. - 8:40 A.M., SEPTEMBER 17, 1862
The final Confederate push against the Cornfield.

The 2nd Massachusetts held Miller's farm house by wrapping itself along the inside of the badly battered picket fence which enclosed the southern and the eastern boundaries of the orchard. The thin slats offered nominal protection from the incoming rounds, but the men were much more secure there than if they had been in the open mow field with the 3rd Wisconsin and the 27th Indiana. Those two approaching Federal regiments did not fire en masse at first for fear of striking down the Ohioans whom they saw darting about in the smoke to their front.

The volley from the 27th Georgia struck the two regiments with a terrible force, but did not rout them. Stubbornly and methodically, the Union soldiers loaded and fired into the smoke to their front while an equally determined enemy replied in kind. Weapons became intolerably hot among the ranks of the 27th Indiana. Skin stuck to rifle barrels and faces were charred from premature discharges. Men were dropping too fast to count. Corporal Edmund Brown (C Co., 27th IN) was stunned by it all. A man near him burst out laughing, following a good shot. A second later, the man dropped. Another soldier turned momentarily to warn the fellow behind him not to fire so close to his face. Both fell, simultaneously.

The file closers faithfully performed their duties. The lines shifted to the center of the regiment as the men closed ranks by stepping sideways over the bodies of their own men.

Wounded soldiers refused to quit the field. A lanky Indiana private was seen staggering from the firing line with what appeared to be a serious wound. After stepping several yards, he turned his back to the fighting (as if to shield himself from another injury) and ripped open his blouse. The resigned expression on his face confirmed his situation. Realizing that he had "bought it", he stoically drawled, "Wall, I guess I'm hurt about as bad as I can be. I believe I'll go back and give 'em some more." He picked up a discarded weapon and walked back to his inevitable death.

Things remained rough. Ammunition was getting very low. The musketry slackened as the men stopped to scrounge cartridges from the dead and the wounded.

Around 8:00 A.M. Major General Joseph Hooker (I Corps) sent Captain Alexander Moore, a volunteer staff aide to Lieutenant William Miller's cavalrymen (H Co., 3rd PA Cav.), who were rounding up stragglers near D. R. Miller's. The captain requested and received ten well mounted men under Corporal Andrew J. Speese. Speese and his people reported to the general as he posted Captain E. W. Matthews' Battery (F, 1st PA) on the eastern end of Miller's mow grass field behind Brigadier General George H. Gordon's Brigade.

Within minutes, Hooker had dispatched all of his newly acquired orderlies, but Speese, to various parts of the field. As Colquitt's attack waxed particularly fierce, the general noted more and more of Gordon's men lying down, perhaps to protect themselves from the terrific musketry.

Hooker yelled at Corporal Speese to send the brigade forward with cold steel and take the Cornfield by the points of its bayonets. The enlisted man rode up to Colonel Thomas Ruger (3rd WI) (whose name he subsequently forgot) and relayed the command.

Colonel Ruger, having assumed command when General Crawford took over the division, refused to comply. His men were almost out of ammunition, he protested. If he was to charge, Hooker would have to deliver the command in person.

The Colonel, in the meantime, asked Colonel George L. Andrews (2nd MA) to commit his men before the 3rd got "used up". Without hesitating, the New Englander ordered his right companies to left wheel into line. His men cleared the fence and swung around on a hinge formed by the left companies. The regiment fired by the right oblique into the left and the center of Colquitt's dwindling brigade. In the East Woods, the 28th Pennsylvania poured a devastating volley into the right rear of the Rebel line.

Notes & Queries

STOP FIVE — Part One

Once you have parked in this area, face the wood line west of the Philadelphia Brigade Monument. The woods to your front represent the actual face of the West Woods. There is a paved path which leads down to an interpretive marker. (This is a tick area.)

As long as you are facing west you can use the reading to interpret the action which occurred here around 9:30 A.M. The Federal troops were inside the woods facing west. Their front line was down along the current Route 65. Their line extended from Starke Avenue (north) to within three hundred feet of Confederate Avenue (south). The action here lasted but a few minutes.

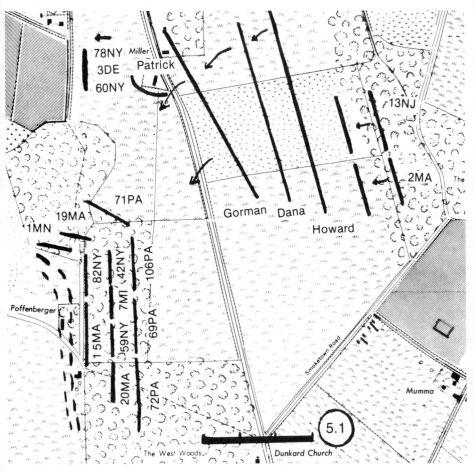

(Map 5.1) 9:00 A.M. - 9:30 A.M., SEPTEMBER 17, 1862
Sedgwick penetrates the West Woods.

The artillery fire and the riflery shredded the Federal ranks. The first volley into Gorman's Brigade gouged huge holes in his line. The 15th Massachusetts, in particular, took a fearful drubbing. Sergeant Johnathan P. Stowe (G Company) fell with a broken right leg. Whatever had hit him had almost unhinged his leg at the knee and he lay helpless on the ground with the shot and the minies singing all about him. Believing death was near, he pulled out his pocket diary and his pencil to leave a testament behind.

"Battle Oh horrid battle," he painfully scrawled, "What sights I have seen. I am wounded! And am afraid shall be again as shells fly past me every few seconds carrying away limbs from the trees..." His body shuddered as he continued, "Am in severe pain. How the shells fly. I do sincerely hope shall not be wounded again."

There were scores of Sergeant Stowes in the 15th Massachusetts.

"Lie down! Every man on his own hook!"

Asa Fletcher (A Co., 15th MA) could hear Captain Saunders' words over and over again. He followed the captain's advice. Fletcher kneeled behind a large oak from which he could see Rebel skirmishers taking cover behind a big haystack to the right of A. Poffenberger's house. The sharpshooter found some courage welling up within him. He cooly counted his rounds — nineteen cartridges. Somehow, the whole business seemed a great deal like target practice. Taking careful aim with his Remington, he deliberately dispatched one Confederate and within a few minutes, he killed four more.

Fletcher's luck ran out as he rammed home his sixth shot. The small bore heated up and fouled, causing the ball to lodge in the barrel before it was properly seated. Without thinking, he stood up, unable to decide whether to extract the bullet or to discharge the piece as it was. For a second, he glanced at the haymound which was less than thirty feet away. He distinctly saw a skirmisher take steady aim and fire.

Fletcher, instinctively, dodged into the round which struck him in the chest. He crashed to the ground, unable to move, numbed from head to foot.

Gorman's Brigade completely blocked the field of fire for the other two brigades. The 19th Massachusetts, which occupied the right of Dana's line, stood on a rise of ground just to the rear of the 1st Minnesota (Gorman's Brigade). The 42nd New York (Dana's Brigade), to its left front, had closed upon the rear of the 1st Minnesota. The 7th Michigan, 59th New York, and the 20th Massachusetts (Dana's Brigade, north to south) continued the line west of the limestone ledge which ran through the woods toward the Dunker Church.

Colonel Hinks ordered the 19th Massachusetts to lie down. The men could not return fire without hitting the Minnesotans. They admired how their colonel sat astride his mount near the center of the regiment with his arms folded across his chest while the bullets and slugs smacked into the trees around him. A smile seemed to flicker on his face as he tempted death.

Death seemed to be everywhere. Twice, the 15th Massachusetts drove away the gunners from one of Stuart's batteries only to be forced back into the West Woods. In all, the New Englanders gained only thirty feet of ground that day. The cornfield north of A. Poffenberger's lent itself to a debacle similar to the one which occurred in the Miller Cornfield. The 15th, which had seen the carnage of the morning's fighting, could also hear its own twenty pound shells rumbling overhead. The gunners across the Antietam were shooting by "guesstimation." They could not see through the pall of smoke which enveloped the West Woods to differentiate friend from foe. They merely placed the shells where they assumed the hostile projectiles came from. Their barrages proved to be unnervingly accurate. Bullets and shrapnel materialized from every quarter.

Notes & Queries

STOP FIVE — Part One — Optional Walking Tour #1

Follow the black paved walkway to the face of the West Woods. On the map it is in the approximate position of "69PA." Follow the paved walkway until it turns back toward the parking lot. Instead of following it back to the parking area, walk into the grassy hollow near the Confederate iron gun. Face south (right) and walk up to the next fence row. At this point the spot marked "72PA" will be on a hill to your right front. (There is a very run down white house near there now.) Take a look around and notice that the Hagerstown Pike is no longer in view. You are standing in the shallow end of a deep ravine. General Jubal Early's brigade came through this ravine and took the 72nd Pennsylvania from the rear, completely unobserved by Federal troops in the Hagerstown Pike.

Riflery splattered the 1st Minnesota. Color Sergeant Samuel Bloomer, who was resting on his flag staff, crumbled to the forest floor when a minie ball penetrated his right leg just below the knee cap. Crawling to the southern side of a big Maryland oak to protect himself from friendly fire, he feverishly tore his trousers off to inspect the wound. The bullet, in exiting, had ripped the back of his leg to a pulp. Bloomer quickly tore a long strip of cloth from his blanket to cut off the blood flow above his knee.

Meanwhile, on the Federal right, the 42nd New York started to scramble up the limestone ledge into the ranks of the 19th Massachusetts. A few men to the south tried to deliberately aim in the direction of Howard's line. About four hundred yards to the left, Captain Oliver W. Holmes, Jr. (A Co., 20th MA) saw an Irishman in G Company face rearward and drop to his knee to shoot. The captain screamed at the man, but he continued to take aim and fire.

"You damn fool!" Holmes shrieked as he struck the soldier with the flat of his sword across the base of the neck and prostrated him.

"What are you doing?" someone exclaimed. "Don't you know any better than to fire into our third line?"

One of the New Yorkers retorted, "You had better look back and see if they are the third line."

Simultaneously, Major Chase Philbrick (15th MA) cried out, "See the Rebels!"

"Bull" Sumner broke off his conversation with Lieutenant Colonel Kimball (15th MA) and shot a startled glance at the ridge where his third line was supposed to be. He followed Philbrick's quaking finger in the direction of the Hagerstown Pike.

Brigadier General Oliver O. Howard, whose men could not see the Confederates through the smoke to their front, saw General Sumner riding frantically toward his brigade.

"My God, we must get out of this!" Sumner shouted but Howard could not hear him above the shooting.

The stunned general wildly signalled Howard to swing his line back by the left flank, and he tried to attempt a turning movement. It was too late. The 72nd Pennsylvania (Birney's Zouaves,

Howard's Brigade) disintegrated and streamed toward the East Woods. The 69th Pennsylvania, while trying to face south, collapsed, which, in turn, broke the 106th and the 71st Pennsylvania regiments. Sumner spurred into the 106th regiment. His eyes flashed and his long white hair streamed out behind him as he waved his hat in the air and called, "Back boys, for God's sake move back; you are in a bad fix." The Pennsylvanians panicked and ran from the field.

Notes & Queries

Proceed back to your vehicle. Drive out to the Hagerstown Pike and turn right. Exit the battlefield to the right onto Route 65 (Sharpsburg Pike), heading north. As you slowly drive north you will see the end of Confederate Avenue to your right. A very short distance beyond there will be the remnants of an old paved driveway on your right. Pull off onto the shoulder at this point and get out of your car. Walk north. Pass the monument to Colonel Stetson of the 58th New York and continue up the hill until you find the monument to the 15th Massachusetts on your right. You are at the spot across from A. Poffenberger's farm on the map. With the monument to your back, look down into the low ground across from you and read the following excerpt.

Return to your car and drive a short distance north to Starke Avenue. Enter the battlefield from this location. At the top of the hill turn right and continue the self guided tour to Stop Six.

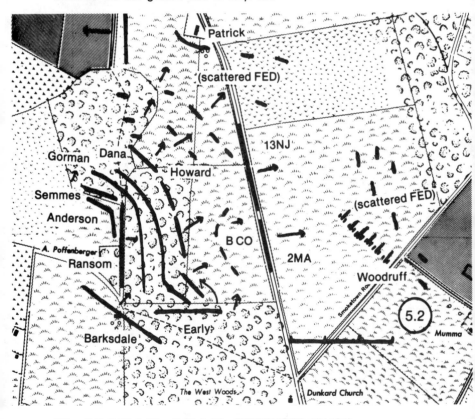

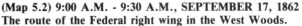

(Map 5.2) 9:00 A.M. - 9:30 A.M., SEPTEMBER 17, 1862
The route of the Federal right wing in the West Woods.

Semmes gave the command to attack. The Confederate regiments hurriedly realigned, mingling commands together. Color Sergeant Bob Forrest (32nd VA) advanced several paces to the front of the outfit and halted to wait upon the rest of the regiment which was still reforming.

Lieutenant Henry St. Clair (I Co.) bolted up to Forrest in a flurry.

"Bob Forrest," St. Clair cried, "why in the hell don't you go forward with the flag; if you won't" — He lunged for it — "give it to me."

Bob gripped the broken staff tighter and snarled back, "You shan't have it; I will carry this flag as far as any man; bring up your line and we will go up together."

While rifle fire peppered the regiment as the men closed ranks, Captain Morrison (15th VA) continually paced the line, rifle in hand, as was customary with many Confederate officers, exhorting his people to keep up their rapid fire. He noticed a very muscular fellow from the 13th North Carolina (Garland's Brigade) clap his mouth in his hands and walk rearward.

The bullet passed through his mouth while he was giving the Rebel yell and missed his teeth. He stumbled through the 15th Virginia mumbling through his clenched teeth, "Boys, I'll have to leave you. Going to the rear to look for that damned ball. Give 'em hell and my compliments."

A little farther down the line a lanky Georgian with a blanket roll with a huge knot in the middle of it halted as the troops regrouped. Slipping the roll off his shoulder, the fellow carefully unrolled the blanket and removed the imposing lump — a half gallon crock of apple butter. The famished soldier scooped the contents out by the handful and shoveled them into his grimy mouth. When the line bolted forward, the Georgian shoved the rest of the apple butter into his mouth and raced into the fray with a dirty face.

Sergeant William H. Andrews (M Co., 1st GA Reg.), who slipped off the top fence rail during Anderson's first advance, picked himself up and nervously "drew trigger" on the color bearer of the 1st Minnesota. Sixty yards to the north, the flag rippled gently in the breeze and the sergeant wanted the singular honor of dropping it. As his sights leveled on the breast of Color Sergeant Samuel Bloomer (1st MN), he fired. Nothing happened! Andrews bitterly fumbled for his nipple wrench and pick. Unscrewing the nipple, he cleaned out the vent at the breech, tapped fresh powder in from another cartridge, replaced the nipple, and recapped. By then, however, the brigade had advanced into the woods.

Lieutenant G. B. Lamar (F Co., 1st GA Reg.) waved his sword from the front of the line, beckoning his men forward. Andrews ran through the ranks to join him lest he be accused of cowardice.

Notes & Queries

STOP SIX — Part One

The parking area is a small pull over on the left near the Mumma Family Cemetery Marker. There is a path to the cemetery. The reading describes an incident in the morning phase of the battle when the Confederates torched the farm house.

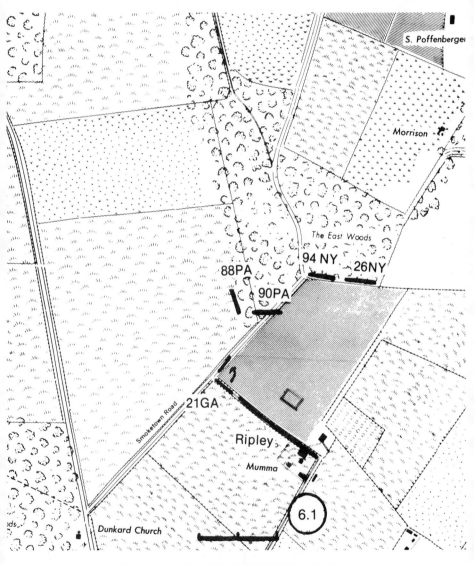

(Map 6.1) 6:25 A.M. - 7:00 A.M., SEPTEMBER 17, 1862
Christian's Brigade stalls Ripley and the 21st Georgia.

Captain James Nisbet (H Co., 21st GA), being the senior captain, immediately assumed command. He ordered the regiment to doublequick toward the left along the Smoketown Road. The rugged Georgians charged in open order toward the first of the two fences which bordered the road when a volley from the East Woods caught them on the front.

Men slumped over the fence rails — dead. Captain Nisbet never saw the bulk of his command scramble into the shallow depression cut by the road. As he swung his legs over the top rail of the worm fence on the southern side of the road, a round struck him square in the gut and sent him flopping into the packed dirt. More bullets kicked up the ground around him. He did not move.

Brigadier General Roswell Ripley, whose regiments held Mumma's lane and orchard, quickly grasped the situation and responded immediately. Colonel William A. Christian's Brigade (the 88th, and 90th PA, and the 26th and 94th NY) having pushed deeper into the East Woods without their commander, who had deserted them for safer ground, tried to blast the socks off the 21st Georgia. It also turned its attention upon Ripley's men.

Outnumbered, Ripley prepared for the worst. While his men fired into the advancing Blue Coats, the general ordered Colonel William L. DeRossett (3rd NC) to torch Mumma's house and barn. He had to deny the Federals any decent cover should he be forced to retire.

(Daniel Mumma, the family's eldest boy, with his younger brother, Samuel, Jr., and their friend had found the house a shambles when they stole into it on the afternoon of the 16th. The place had been ransacked. Sam and the other boy left Dan alone in the house that night.

Dan had bolted the door to discourage any further looting. Shortly after Sam left, he slipped through an open window on the ground floor and hid in the upper level of the spring house. By daylight on the 17th, he was long gone.)

Sergeant Major James Clarke and six other "volunteers" from A Company, 3rd North Carolina, pounded furiously against the door of the house. It would not budge. Bullets chinked brick fragments off the wall around the detachment. Armed only with torches from their morning cook fires, the seven Rebels felt very insecure. As they slipped around to a protected side of the house, they discovered the open window which Dan Mumma had forgotten to close during his escape.

One of the men flipped his torch into the empty room, while Clarke took the rest of the party toward the barn. A bullet struck the sergeant major in the arm, but did not drop him. He finished his assignment and returned his men, unscathed, to the regiment before he reported to Ripley, who immediately sent him with orders to the 4th and 44th Georgia regiments (Ripley's left regiments).

Notes & Queries

STOP SIX — Part Two

Using Map 6.2, orient yourself by facing toward the Mumma farm house. The Roulette farm is to the southeast in another hollow and marks the position of the 27th North Carolina and the 3rd Arkansas.

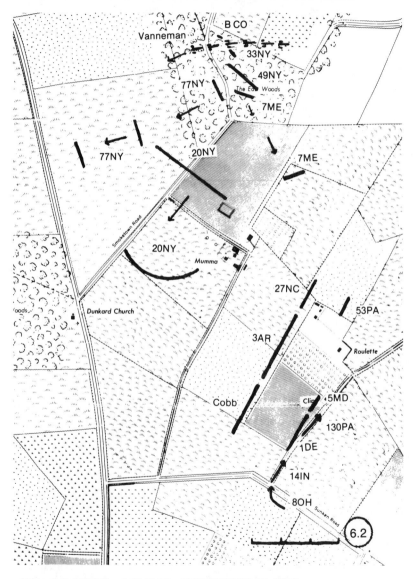

(Map 6.2) NOON - 1:00 P.M., SEPTEMBER 17, 1862
Irwin's Brigade, VI Corps, flanks Cooke and Cobb in Mumma's swale.

The small 7th Maine regiment left wheeled, pushed through the woods, and broke into Mumma's plowed field north of the family cemetary. One by one, the men feverishly tore down each fence rail in their path as they worked their way toward the left flank of the 27th North Carolina.

Colonel Cooke, who finally realized that his terribly out-numbered soldiers could not withstand the odds, hollered at his men to pull back. The Rebels, who heard the order, fired one last volley into the fast approaching 20th New York, then panicked and "double-quick timed" (according to Captain James Graham, G Co.) back toward their original position — right into the waiting and leveled weapons of a large number of their armed "prisoners" who had decided to "unquit" the war.

The 3rd Arkansas came to a sudden halt as the regrouped Federals in Roulette's lane leveled their weapons and fired into them. Men slammed to the ground by squads. Fred Worth-ington (A Co.) collapsed next to Captain Bart Johnson — dead. Within seconds, about half the regiment was down.

Bullets now came in from all directions, in many instances at ranges under sixty yards as the 27th North Carolina and the 3rd Arkansas retreated directly across the front of the 20th New York, which was too busy charging toward the guns along the Hagerstown Pike to pay any attention to them.

Major Hyde (7th ME) saw the bulk of the frightened Rebs break across his front — east to west — at a safe distance from his struggling troops and decided to liberally interpret Captain Long's directive to connect with Von Vegesack's left flank. The major sent his soldiers scrambling southeast into the Cornfield to roust the Confederates lingering in Roulette's buildings, an action which cost him twelve men and a few minutes.

Meanwhile, the rest of Irwin's mishandled brigade stampeded into combat. The four hundred man 49th New York swung left and followed on the rear of the 20th New York at about one hun-dred yards. The regiment stepped into the clover field south of the Smoketown Road at the double quick with their muskets at the right shoulder shift and sprayed around Mumma's burned out barn where some comrades from the 21st New York (Patrick's Brigade, I Corps) called after them, "You will find a hot time of it in there, boys!"

The 33rd New York (about one hundred fifty men) which brought up the tail end of the column, stumbled into line on the left rear, less B Company which Vanneman's Battery (B, MD) cut off from the regiment as it passed through the line en route to the Cornfield.

The very disorganized brigade raced through a rain of exploding shells toward the western most section of the Bloody Lane. About half way through Mumma's swale, Captain Long, at General William F. Smith's request, ordered the 33rd New York away from the left flank of the 49th New York. Lieutenant Colonel Joseph W. Corning faced his command by the right flank and double quicked them toward the right flank of the 49th New York, which threw it across the Hagerstown Pike into the West Woods, immediately south of the Dunker Church.

Notes & Queries

STOP SEVEN

The parking area is a small pull over on the left of the road opposite the Visitors' Center. The reading and the map refer to the fighting which occurred around the guns in the hollow behind the Visitors' Center. This action happened almost simultaneously with the event described at the West Woods.

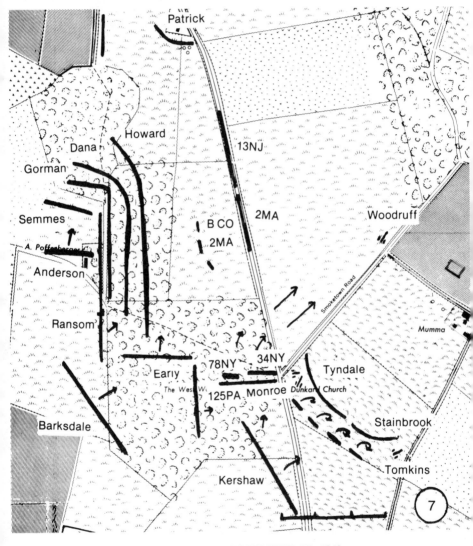

(Map 7) 9:00 A.M. - 9:30 A.M., SEPTEMBER 17, 1862
The collapse of the Dunker Church and the envelopment of Sedgwick's flank.

Tyndale's Ohioans, to the rear of Monroe, prepared for the onslaught. A projectile exploded in the center of the 5th Ohio's color guard. The men quickly raised the standards as the brigade instinctively rose to its feet along the crest and fixed bayonets. Tyndale's line took aim as the South Carolinians neared the guns. At twenty-five yards, they fired. Kershaw's Brigade staggered, held for a few moments, then slowly retired to the West Woods, where joined by Ransom's Brigade, they advanced a second time.

At that moment, Brigadier General George Greene (Tyndale's Division commander) raced onto the field with Captain John A. Tompkins' Battery (A, 1st Rhode Island). The Ohioans cheered as Greene rushed the battery through the left of the line and posted the pieces to meet Kershaw's assault. The general rose in the stirrups and raised his hat to them.

Kershaw's people started to close again on the Mumma farm. The brave Confederates charged across the Pike right into the muzzles of the two batteries and another wall of flaming lead sent them reeling back to the West Woods. As the smoke cleared and that sector of the battlefield quieted, the Federal soldiers stared in horror across the open ground to their front. The Confederate dead, mostly men from the 3rd and the 7th South Carolina regiments, lay in windrows in front of Monroe's and Tompkins' smoking guns. The colors of the 7th South Carolina, having been shot from their staff, were draped across the still warm corpse of the last member of the color guard. Kershaw sacrificed over half of his men in the attack.

Wounded men writhed upon the ground. Private Tresse (B Co., 125th PA) waited until the last Confederate trampled over him before he picked himself up from among the dead and casually ambled back to his regiment. Private Fred Gerhard (D Co.) scrounged over the corpses behind the battery looking for a new weapon. He "swapped" his piece for a nicer one. While he was at it, he "appropriated" a leather case, containing a knife, fork, and spoon, from a dead Reb, whose eating days were over. He heard a wounded Rebel call out to him. Gerhard asked him what he wanted. The man asked to be put in the shade. Gerhard helped him to his feet and tried to carry the man off. When he discovered, however, that the Reb could not walk because he was partially disemboweled, he laid him back down. He saw no use in dragging a dying man to safety. Many other soldiers spent the lull in the fighting to collect souvenirs.

One of Tompkins' sergeants shaved the fried brains of a dead Confederate from the muzzle of Thomas A. Aldrich's cannon and kept them for a momento. Aldrich who was unable to leave his gun, dejectedly watched Corporal Jacob Orth (D Co.), whose regiment, the 28th Pennsylvania (with the 111th Pennsylvania) had defended Tompkins' right section from Kershaw's attack, unwrap the standard of the 7th South Carolina from the corpse of the last bearer. (His action won him the Medal of Honor four years later.)

Notes & Queries

STOP EIGHT

When proceeding to Stop Eight do not veer off onto the paved lane to your left, as you ascend the first hill, while heading toward the tower on the eastern end of the Bloody Lane. Continue straight over that ridge and use the parking spaces in the low ground to your left. There is a paved walk which leads to a stone wall and an overlook north of this lot. The fighting in the Bloody Lane lasted from 9:30 A.M. until around noon. The events described in this excerpt occurred on the high ground to your left where the number "6" is on this map and extended to the tower on your right. (The tower is a postwar structure). You are standing in what was a cornfield. On this map it is near the back of the arrow to the right of the number "2." (This is a tick area and the gnats are terrible in the spring and summer.)

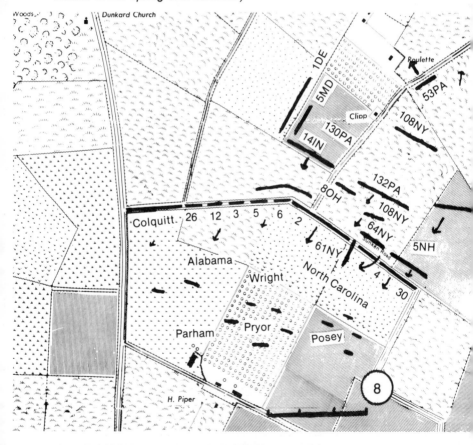

(Map 8) NOON - 1:00 P.M., SEPTEMBER 17, 1862
The Bloody Lane collapses.

Lieutenant Colonel J. N. Lightfoot (6th AL) haled over Brigadier General Robert E. Rodes as he approached the regiment's left wing from the mow grass south of the lane. Lightfoot gestured toward his enfiladed right wing, which was masked by the northwestern corner of Piper's cornfield. Rodes impatiently yelled at Lightfoot to pull his right wing out of the road into the corn, then galloped back toward Piper's farm without waiting to see the command executed.

J. N. Lightfoot stepped behind the center of the skeletal regiment and called, "6th Alabama, about face, forward march."

As the powder stained survivors leaped and clawed their way over the bank behind them into the corn, Major E. L. Hobson, commanding the 5th Alabama, on Lightfoot's left, rushed over and asked if the whole brigade was to retire. Lightfoot, having misunderstood the original command in the din of the battle, merely replied, "Yes."

One by one, first in squads, then by platoons, Rodes' five regiments shattered and streamed rearward. The general, who did not know what had transpired until it was too late, had fallen with a canister shot in the thigh while tending a wounded aide.

The 130th Pennsylvania rose up and pursued the Rebels into the lane, while the 64th/61st New York stood up and right wheeled, throwing its left flank into the lane between the 4th North Carolina and the 14th North Carolina. The New Yorkers literally jumped over the heads of the Confederates. Quickly, they unpiled the corpses and laid each man out individually then handed their canteens to the wounded Confederates.

Part of the 108th New York plunged into the lane, trampling dead and wounded Confederates under them. Rebel and Yankee troops became too entangled to get clear fields of fire. The North Carolinians could not hold the lane any longer. Those who could broke and ran through the corn south of the road. Bullets and canister gouged the Confederates from the north and the east. Men dropped rapidly. Others were brutally hurled through the corn. Commands disintegrated into frightened and confused squads. (The regiment lost two hundred seventy-eight of five hundred twenty-three officers and men engaged.)

On the far left, the 5th New Hampshire bolted ahead of the rest of its brigade toward the Bloody Lane. As they swept forward, the New Englanders shot down the remaining Confederates, who were rapidly throwing down their weapons and falling to their knees with their hands raised.

Lieutenant Thomas Livermore (K Co.) thought they had killed them to a man when one of the Rebs, who was playing "opossum", sprang up from among the corpses and dashed for the rail fence behind him. Shots followed him and he slumped dead over the top rail. As the 5th New Hampshire pushed a short distance into Piper's cornfield, the lieutenant had to urge several men forward. They lagged behind to maliciously shoot and bayonet the already bullet riddled corpse. The rest of the men crouched among the bloodied cornstalks and were blindly shooting through the low hanging smoke toward the rapidly disappearing Confederate line.

Notes & Queries

STOP EIGHT — Optional Walking Tour #1

Walk down into the deepest portion of the lane. Turning left, go to the top of the hill where the monument to the 130th Pennsylvania stands. Robert Rodes' Alabama brigade held the fence row from where you are standing to the corner of Mumma's Lane. Head west into the low ground then face right (north). Mumma's Lane will be on the rise to your left. The following reading describes the encounter between the Alabamians and the 1st Delaware when the Federals attempted to retrieve their downed colors. It also describes part of the action illustrated on Map 8 when the 61st/64th New York closed to within thirty feet of the lane.

Second Lieutenant Charles B. Tanner (H Co., 1st DE) did not care about the fighting in Mumma's swale to the right of his regiment. He had other things on his mind. The regimental colors were still on the ground sixty feet in front of the Confederates. Major Thomas A. Smyth (1st DE) offered to gather up twenty-five of the regiment's best shots and instruct them to fire above the colors if Tanner would run forward to snatch them up.

"Do it," Tanner cried, "and I will get there!"

Twenty volunteers responded to Tanner's call and sprang with him into the bullet sprayed open ground. As he reached the colors and tugged them free of the standard bearer's corpse, he ruefully noticed they were splattered with blood. A second later, a minie ball shattered his right arm. Not waiting for another wound, he clenched the flag in his bloodied right hand and set the record for the eighty yard dash. Two more bullets slammed into his body but did not drop him. He staggered into the regiment as it prepared for Cooke's charge against its right flank. Major Smyth immediately promoted the profusely bleeding Tanner to first lieutenant then ordered the regiment to pull back its right flank to meet the Confederate attack.

At the bend in the Bloody Lane, for the last ten minutes, Barlow's two New York regiments (61st/64th NY) had brutally pinned the 4th North Carolina. The New Yorkers kept the Rebs down but not without problems of their own. Private Barney Rogers, an Irishman (A Co., 61st NY) went into combat with a worn out strap for a belt. When the regiment crawled over the fence northeast of the lane to engage the Rebels, his "belt" snapped. Unable to hold onto his pants, and simultaneously, load and fire, he released his grip on the waistband. The trousers fell down around his ankles and hobbled him like a horse.

As his sergeant, Charles Fuller (C Co.), paced the line in performance of his duties as file closer, Barney called over his shoulder, "Charley, cut the damned things off!" Fuller pulled out his large pocket knife and slit the pants from waist band to ankle on one side.

"You can kick the other leg out," Fuller shouted.

A few jiggles later, and the Irishman was in the fight unhindered. A southerly breeze cleared the smoke along the regiment's front and sent the Irishman's shirt tail flapping in its wake. Laughter echoed in the air behind Barney Rogers when Sergeant Fuller hauled aside Captain Ike Plumb (C Co.) to gawk at his bare backside. The illiterate private was naked from his socks to his waist.

Captain William Graham's Battery (K, 1st U.S.) fired over and into the Confederate line from the eastern corner of the lane. The Rebels' fire slackened perceptibly with every artillery discharge. They started to waver, particularly in the 2nd North Carolina, which held the ascending ground in the apex of the Bloody Lane. Orderly Sergeant James Shinn (B Co., 4th NC), whose regiment occupied the line two regiments to the east wondered how much longer his men could endure the small arms and the gunnery fire which pounded the regiment from all directions but the rear.

Notes & Queries

STOP EIGHT — Optional Walking Tour #2

Turn to the right and walk to the brow of the hill where the monument to the 130th Pennsylvania stands. When you scan the horizon to the northeast and refer to the map to the positions marked "132PA" and "108NY" you will see how the Federals along that ridge could enfilade the Confederates from the right.

Continue into the low ground, heading toward the tower on the far eastern end of the lane. When you reach the high ground near the tower turn around, facing south and southwest and read the following excerpt. It describes the final moments in the lane when the 5th New Hampshire repulsed a Confederate counterattack.

A cry bounced off Charles Fuller's (C Co., 61st NY) head. Turning about, the sergeant watched the bare buttocked Private Barney Rogers (A Co.) crawl off the field like a wounded dog. The middle aged Irishman clumsily stumbled away on two hands and one leg. The other, he kept extended full length behind him. (Unknown to Fuller, a ball glanced off a rock beneath Rogers' foot and bounced upward through the private's big toe.)

As Richardson's men retreated through the corn their lines became entangled. On the far left, the 5th New Hampshire split into two wings and was nearly flanked by Hill's small party.

Colonel Edward Cross angrily regrouped his New Englanders below the muzzles of William Graham's twelve pound Napoleons (K, 1st U.S.), which were firing ineffectively toward the high ground south of the Dunker Church. Thomas Livermore (K Co.) peered through the smoke, which engulfed the regiment, trying to pinpoint the Confederates who had rushed under Graham's guns to a fence several yards south of the line (along the far border of the cornfield). As the 5th New Hampshire stepped backwards through the corn toward the lane, Colonel Cross separated it from the troops to the right and reunited the two wings.

Once in the lane with the rest of the brigade, the 5th New Hampshire knelt on the bloodied Confederate corpses and braced themselves for a counterattack. They could see little movement through the tall corn. Presently, a sharp eyed soldier cried aloud that the Rebs were moving in on the regiment from the left. Bending his regiment at right angles, facing east and south, Edward Cross filed part of his command to the left and counterflanked the Confederates.

A terrible firefight erupted at point blank range. Artillery shells from the far southern ridge above Piper's farm exploded indiscriminately in the mass of writhing soldiers. A single burst in G Company killed or wounded eight of the nine men in the 5th New Hampshire's color guard. Simultaneously, the Rebels dashed for the third successive time into the muzzles of the Federal line.

Lieutenant Livermore felt the blood in the lane ooze into his knees. A darting glance to the right, where the fighting still raged unabated, told him that no help would come from that quarter.

"Shoot the man with the flag!"

The shout echoed emptily in the lieutenant's ears. Less than fifteen yards away, a Confederate standard bearer, who was semaphoring the colors from side to side, disappeared in a burst of riflery.

Colonel Cross, bare headed, his wounded scalp still streaming red through his red bandana and down over his powder stained face, maniacally paced his line.

"Put on the war paint!" he screamed.

The New Englanders tore open cartridges and smeared their sweating faces with powder before loading.

"Give 'em the war whoop!" the colonel blustered.

Shrieking and chattering like lunatics, the soldiers of the 5th New Hampshire began firing rapidly into the corn. Screams, curses, and yelps reverberated in their sector of the field.

"Fire! Fire! Fire faster!" some men prattled.

Thomas Livermore got caught up in the madness. Searching the ground around him, he pried a Belgian musket from the waxen hands of the Rebel corpse beneath him. A quick inspection showed him the antique was capped and probably loaded.

Despite orders to the contrary, the lieutenant snapped the smoothbore to his shoulder and pulled the trigger. He liked it. The thrill of a musket recoiling into his shoulder invigorated him. He dropped to all fours and started hunting for another piece when Colonel Cross stepped into his path.

Cross boomed, "Mister Livermore, tend to your company!"

The lieutenant quickly obeyed.

The 132nd Pennsylvania, which had remained on the slope during that final charge, heard a louder ruckus from the rear. Once again, General Thomas Meagher, aboard his white charger, led his men at the double-quick toward the Bloody Lane.

As the general neared the Pennsylvanians' left flank, he toppled from the saddle. Getting to his feet, he staggered and reeled about, "swearing like a crazy man", Adjutant Hitchcock (132nd PA) wrote. (The enlisted men insisted that Meagher was drunk.)

STOP NINE

If there is anyone in your party who is in poor health, who has heart or respiratory problems or who is physically disabled, park at the base of the hill near Burnside Bridge in the space that is marked for specially tagged vehicles. The path to the bridge is gravel paved and can be rather hard to negotiate. (Remember to watch out for wasps in the hand rails near the bridge. Keep an eye out for black snakes. They like to sun on the bank near the creek. This area is a tick area.)

This reading is best done under the shade of the large mulberry tree near the mouth of the bridge on the eastern bank. The incident which is described transpired behind this tree next to the bridge. The Confederate position was on the hillside on the western bank of the creek.

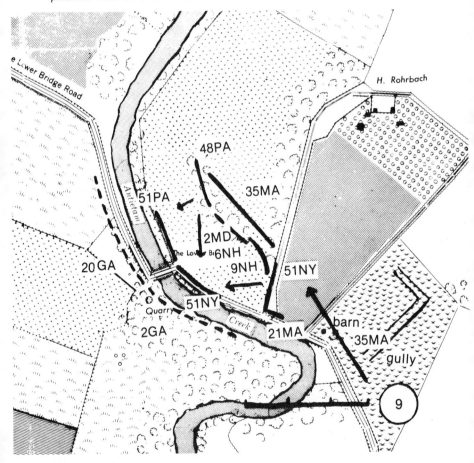

(Map 9) NOON - 1:00 P.M., SEPTEMBER 17, 1862
The 51st Pennsylvania and the 51st New York gain a foothold at the Lower Bridge.

From behind the knolls, Colonel Ferrero, who had caught up with the 35th Massachusetts, could not understand why the 51st Pennsylvania had not crossed the stream as ordered. The dapper dancing master impatiently ordered the ever present John Hudson to go down and find out why Colonel Hartranft had not done as commanded. The fact that their own artillery might destroy the advancing column apparently never occurred to him. He simultaneously detached A Company from the right of the 35th to assist the left flank of the 21st Massachusetts.

Lieutenant Hudson glanced about as he, pursuant to the colonel's desire, started down the slight valley toward Hartranft's pinned soldiers. Members of the 2nd Maryland and the 6th New Hampshire fired sporadically toward the creek. Colonel Enoch Fellows (9th NH) periodically poked his head over the sparsely wooded crest to observe the fighting. While he bobbed about, his head protected from the bright sun by a palm leaf hat, his tiring soldiers, for the most part, kept their skulls below the line of fire. Before he trotted into the corn stubbled valley, the normally cautious John Hudson asked the New Englanders, some of whom hid too much for his liking, not to shoot him in the back.

Taking off at a steady trot, the lieutenant dashed into the line just south of the bridge. The men pointed him in the direction of the northern parapet. Hudson darted across the bridge's mouth, stooping low to keep his back well beneath the road crest in the middle of the bridge. Prone Pennsylvanians, who were using the road hump for cover, busily peppered the west bank with a steady fusillade. He found Colonel Hartranft and his color guard huddled below the north wing of the bridge wall. As the aide approached the colonel, a "drop short" from Simmond's Battery exploded in the creek and sprayed water over the men behind the stone wall.

Hudson screamed at the colonel, ordering him to cross the bridge.

"Does he desire it?" Hartranft incredulously shouted back.

"Yes, sir," Hudson replied.

"Very well," Hartranft replied.

The two officers headed south together. Hartranft and his color guard worked their way into the crowd on the bridge while

Hudson sought out Colonel Robert B. Potter (51st NY) and told him to follow the Pennsylvanians across. Potter shouted at his men to move and bolted onto the parapet where he was seen standing atop one of the walls cursing and swearing like a madman. Lieutenant Hudson hurriedly raced back to the safety of the knolls. As he explained it later, "having on straps & sword & pistol, I was willing to keep moving," lest he be found too close to the bridge should the assault fail or should some Confederate sharpshooter single him out as a prize target. At the moment, the Confederates had more than one stray Yankee lieutenant to worry about.

Colonel Henry L. Benning, commanding the Georgians at the bridgehead, found his position, which his soldiers had so valiantly held for so long, becoming more untenable. For no apparent reason to Benning, the 50th Georgia disappeared from his immediate right flank (which, perhaps, explains why the 35th Massachusetts received no incoming fire at the creek bend). The morning attacks left his men physically exhausted. Their fire dwindled perceptibly as the Yankees down at the bridge began to stir. Benning's good fortune had run its course along with his ammunition supply. He started to pass the word along the crest to fall back.

They managed to drag away some of their wounded as they retreated, including one of them whom they should have left behind to die. The Georgians refused to abandon the gut shot Johnnie Slade (H Co.). (He died four days later in Sharpsburg.)

Part of D Company of the 2nd Georgia did not hear the command above the crashing of the Federal artillery fire. Benning immediately sent First Sergeant Henean H. Perry (D Co., 2nd GA) to retrieve the rest of the command. He arrived as the company shot away its last rounds of ammunition.

Notes & Queries

STOP NINE — Optional Walking Tour

Follow the fence row along the creek to the south until you come to an opening in the fence. Go through the opening past the iron marker. There will be a small knoll in front of you. Follow the contour of the knoll to the left until you come to a cleared path which will lead up to the monument of the 11th Connecticut. Burnside Bridge Road will run around the knoll to the south. This spot marks the starting point for the first attack (10:00 A.M.) against the bridge.

The Lower Bridge

Lieutenant Colonel William R. Holmes (2nd GA, Toombs'
BG, D. R. Jones' Div.) vowed to "Stonewall" Jackson that his
men would hold the heights overlooking the Lower Bridge or
die in a ditch trying. The Confederates, though short on men,
had more than their share of determination. The 2nd Georgia
(about 125 men) and the 20th Georgia (225 men) held the heights
along the creek and the Lower Bridge Road for about eight hundred seventy-five yards, which placed one man about every eight
feet. Richardson's and Eshelman's Batteries covered the
Georgians from a ridge about five hundred yards west of the
bridge. The 50th Georgia (210 men), with one company from
Jenkins' South Carolina Brigade and a battalion (five companies)
from the 11th Georgia (G. T. Anderson's BG) occupied the bluffs
from the right of the 2nd Georgia, at the quarry, south to the
big bend in the creek, then west to a spot directly north of Snave-
ly's Ford. The distance of over one thousand six hundred fifty
yards greatly strained their defensive capabilities. They, probably, numbered a little over three hundred men. Benning's
(Toombs') Brigade, which normally had two other regiments with
it, had left the 15th and the 17th Georgia with the other half of
the 11th Georgia on provost duty with the Army's wagon train
on the Virginia side of the Potomac. The Georgians took cover
behind trees, rock outcroppings, and fences along the bridge
road and the western bank of the creek. Many shinnied up trees
to cover the bridge from better vantage points.

By 9:00 A.M., they had repulsed the cautious probe by two
companies of the 11th Ohio. An hour later, the 11th Connecticut, under the command of Colonel Henry W. Kingsbury, was
sent from Harland's Brigade (Rodman's Div., IX) against the
bridge. The Yankees burst over the twin knolls east of the bluffs
in extended order. Benning's Georgians fired madly into the
onrushing Yankees as they reached the rail fence and the stone
wall to the south and the north of the bridge, respectively. For
ten minutes the New Englanders put out a tremendous fusillade.
Their men lay sprawled about the stubble field behind them.
Others were draped over the stone wall.

Captain John Griswold (A Co., 11th CT) leaped the stone wall, followed by several men and plunged into the creek only to find it swift flowing and four feet deep in the center. A burst of small arms fire caught the party there. A few men plunged into the stream — dead. The others, Griswold excepted, turned back. The captain, who was already mortally wounded, staggered to the Confederate side of the creek where he collapsed on the muddy bank and bled to death.

The Georgians forced the New Englanders back to the safety of the knolls. They inflicted one hundred thirty-nine casualties upon the Yankees, including their colonel, who left the field — dying. He perished at the hands of men under the command of his beloved brother-in-law, Brigadier General David R. Jones. The Confederates let their heated gun barrels cool and saved their rapidly depleting ammunition supply for further assaults.

Notes & Queries

STOP TEN

This part of the tour road is represented on the map by the fence row which parallels the dashed line labeled "Archer," "Georgia," and "Branch." You are parked opposite the Otto farm. The reading portrays the situation at dark as the fighting ended for the day in the hollow before you. The 35th Massachusetts was along the treeline to your right front.

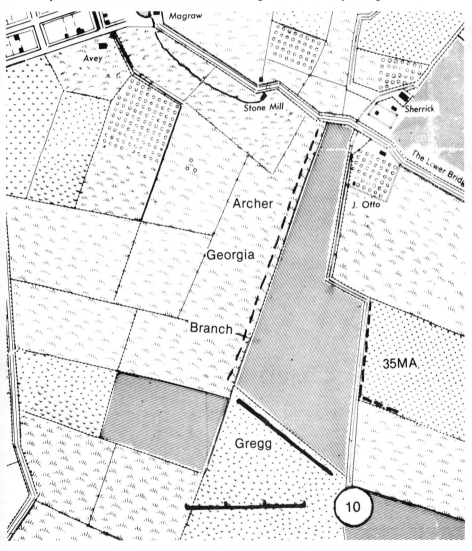

(Map 10) 4:20 P.M. - DARK, SEPTEMBER 17, 1862
The 35th Massachusetts shows its mettle.

The cornered 35th Massachusetts bore the brunt of the Confederate counterattack with Lieutenant John N. Coffin's section. The Rebel artillery seemed to concentrate on the regiment, which, numbering around eight hundred men, must have appeared as large as a brigade. The New Englanders went prone and returned fire as fast as they could. File closers and line officers, pursuant to regulations, remained upright and tended to their lines. Following the first disorganized volley, the shooting devolved to firing at will.

Ramrods clattered fitfully down bores. Men cursed between rounds. Others screamed when they were hit. A sulfuric cloud enveloped the entire position. A bullet ripped through Lieutenant Colonel Carruth's neck very close to the jugular vein. Captain Stephen H. Andrews (A Co.), senior captain, immediately took over as Carruth staggered up the hill toward the bridge.

On the left, in K Company, all three officers were wounded. Over fifty percent of the company's sixty men were casualties, among them Privates Roscoe Bradley, who had boasted before going into action that he would come out unscathed, and his comrade, Sergeant William N. Meserve. They dropped simultaneously.

"Meserve I'm hit," Bradley blurted.

"So am I," shouted Meserve, as two bullets struck him in quick succession in the left arm.

Seconds later, Bradley cried, "Meserve I'm killed."

He collapsed, dead, in his sergeant's arms. The sergeant quietly put his friend down and started to tie off his arm above the elbow.

At one point, Captain William S. King (K Co.), the acting major, picked up a musket and shot at a cluster of Confederate flags behind the stone wall. His men cheered him feebly. They were too busy to worry about an officer's bravado.

Rifle barrels overheated. Forestocks smoldered. Cartridges jammed partway down fouled bores but the men triggered the pieces anyway without properly seating the bullets. They fired at every opportunity. Being "green," their officers did not have the sense to retire when common sense dictated to do so.

By dusk, as the casualties mounted and ammunition became harder to find, the regiment's rate of fire diminished perceptibly. Captains John Lathrop (I Co.) and William King (K Co.), who was severely wounded, crawled among the dead and injured, scrounging for cartridges. Above the racket they occasionally heard Captain Tracy Cheever (C Co.) advising his people to, "Pop away! boys, Pop away!" The left wing continued to get pounded mercilessly, while the right, under the protection of Coffin's section, took fewer hits.

Notes & Queries

STOP ELEVEN

If you stop next to the artillery piece near the northeast corner of the cemetery wall and face east, you will be looking down the Boonsboro Pike, much as Lee's artillerists did throughout most of the day. The only cavalry charge which took place during the battle occurred near the crest of the large hill directly opposite you. The map shows what happened on the other side of that hill as the 4th Pennsylvania Cavalry attempted to pierce the Confederate center between noon and 1:00 P.M. The line represented by "Hains," "Tidball," and "Gibson" indicates the crest of that ridge.

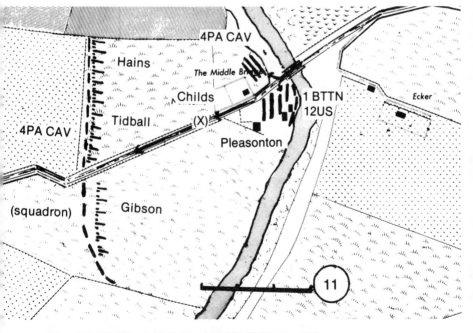

(Map 11) NOON - 1:00 P.M., SEPTEMBER 17, 1862
The 4th Pennsylvania Cavalry and the Federal horse artillery go into action at the Middle Bridge.

Lieutenant Thomas Evans (D and E Cos., 1st Bttn., 12th U.S.) stayed with his men by the Middle Bridge while four batteries of the 2nd U.S. Horse Artillery swung into action on the ridge about five hundred yards from the creek. Captain John C. Tidball's gunners (A Btty.) with Lieutenant Peter C. Hains (M Batty.) roared away from the northern side of the Boonsboro Pike while Captain Horatio Gibson's batteries (C and G) opened upon the Confederates along the pike near Sharpsburg. The ground literally heaved and rolled as the artillerists hurled shell after shell toward the village. Simultaneously, a squadron of the 4th Pennsylvania Cavalry conducted an insane charge across the Middle Bridge toward the valley beyond the artillery pieces. Several rounds struck the column about one hundred yards west of the span, killling its colonel, Benjamin Childs, and knocking down the better part of the squadron. The cavalrymen behind it hastily dismounted. Shaken troopers unsnapped their carbines and, using their horses for cover, slowly edged their way toward the ravine in front of the batteries. While the rest of the 4th Pennsylvania filed into the field to the right of the Pike, the remainder of Brigadier General Alfred Pleasonton's Cavalry Division wheeled left and right and filled the low ground along the creek.

Within fifteen minutes, the Pennsylvanians' skirmishers came under what they considered severe riflery from three of Nathan Evans' South Carolina regiments (18th, 22nd, and 23rd SC), which commanded a Virginia rail fence between two plowed fields on a ridge seven hundred fifty yards from Tidball's and Hains' Batteries. The cavalrymen held their ground and spread out in an extended arch which conformed to the huge swale from Newcomer's house almost to the creek bank.

Minutes after a shell fragment knocked him down, Lieutenant Warren Pursley (G Co., 18th SC) regained his senses. Soldiers streamed past him. He could not walk. Every breath hurt him severely. "Bullets pouring about like hail. Shells bursting round and over me. Throwing dirt on me," he recalled. "Looked impossible to escape." He lay there waiting to die.

Captain Tidball (A, 2nd U.S.) began complaining to the Regulars across the creek that he needed more support. He would have to wait. V Corps commander, Major General Fitz Porter, apparently had made it clear to his divisional officers that he needed them where they were. They had to keep the Middle Bridge from falling into Confederate hands.

Captain Charles W. Squires (1st Co., Washington Artillery — LA), whose battery was on the first ridge immediately west of the Federal horse artillery, was taking fire from three directions — north, east, and south. The position seemed untenable. He felt isolated and hopeless. Below the ridge, west of his guns, Garnett's pitiful excuse for a brigade huddled, not daring to rise into the Federals' line of sight. The Yankees were shelling the position very severely.

To worsen matters, Robert E. Lee had insisted on hanging around his position for what seemed, to the captain, like the better part of the day. The commanding general was piqued while he surveyed the front east and north of the Middle Bridge.

"Captain, our men are acting badly," Lee grumbled.

Notes & Queries

Notes & Queries